Kubernetes
Tutorial for Beginners

Christian Leornardo

TABLE OF CONTENTS

Introduction 1

    Audience..1
    Prerequisites...1

Overview 2

    Features of Kubernetes 2

Architecture 3

    Cluster Architecture 3
    Master Machine Components...........................3
        etcd..3
        API Server 4
        Controller Manager 4
        Scheduler..4
    Node Components...5
        Docker..5
        Kubelet Service 5
        Kubernetes Proxy Service 5
    Master and Node Structure.............................5

Setup 7

    Prerequisites...7
    Install Docker Engine 8
    Install etcd 2.0 8
    Configure kube-apiserver 11
    Configure the kube Controller Manager 11
    Kubernetes Node Configuration.......................11

Images..14

Jobs 16

    Creating a Job 16
    Scheduled Job...17

Labels & Selectors 19

    Labels...19

Selectors 19
    Set-based Selectors 19

Namespace..21

  Functionality of Namespace 21
  Create a Namespace..21
  Control the Namespace..21
  Using Namespace in Service - Example 22

Node..23

  Service with Selector 23
  Node Controller...24

Service 25

  Service without Selector...25
  Service Config File with Selector 25
  Multi-Port Service Creation 26
  Types of Services 26

Pod 28

  Types of Pod 28
    Single Container Pod 28
    Multi Container Pod 29

Replication Controller 30

  Setup Details 30

Replica Sets 32

  Setup Details 33

Deployments 34

  Changing the Deployment..34
  Deployment Strategies 34
  Create Deployment 35
  Fetch the Deployment...35
  Check the Status of Deployment..35
  Updating the Deployment...36
  Rolling Back to Previous Deployment.................................36

Volumes 37

Types of Kubernetes Volume 37
Persistent Volume and Persistent Volume Claim 39
Creating Persistent Volume 39
Creating PV 40
Checking PV 40
Describing PV 40
Creating Persistent Volume Claim 41
Creating PVC 41
Getting Details About PVC 41
Describe PVC..41
Using PV and PVC with POD 42

Secrets...43

Creating From Text File..43
Creating From Yaml File 43
Creating the Secret 43
Using Secrets 44
As Environment Variable 44
As Volume..44
Secret Configuration As Environment Variable 44
Secrets As Volume Mount 45

Network Policy 46

Network Policy Yaml...46

API 48

Adding API to Kubernetes..48
API Changes...48
API Versioning 50
Alpha Level 50
Beta Level 50
Stable Level 50

Kubectl 51

Setting Kubectl 51
On Linux 51
On OS X workstation...51

Configuring Kubectl 51
   Verifying the Setup 52

Kubectl Commands 53
   kubectl config view 56

Creating an App...62
   By Downloading...62
   From Docker File...63

App Deployment 65
   Ngnix Load Balancer Yaml File 65
   Ngnix Replication Controller Yaml 66
   Frontend Service Yaml File 67
   Frontend Replication Controller Yaml File....................67
   Backend Service Yaml File...68
   Backed Replication Controller Yaml File 68

Autoscaling...70
   Environment Variable 70

Dashboard Setup...73
   Setting Up the Dashboard 73
   Installing Python...73
   Installing GCC...73
   Installing make..73
   Installing Java...73
   nstalling Node.js 74
   Installing gulp...74
   Verifying Versions...74
   Installing GO 74
   Installing Kubernetes Dashboard 75
   Running the Dashboard...75

Monitoring 77
   Monitoring with Prometheus...77
   Sematext Docker Agent...77
   Deploying Agents to Nodes 78
   Configuring SemaText Docker Agent.............................78

Create DaemonSet Object...78
    Running the Sematext Agent Docker with kubectl.......79
Kubernetes Log...79
Using ELK Stack and LogSpout...80
Creating Replication Controller 80
Kibana URL 82

INTRODUCTION

Kubernetes is a container management technology developed in Google lab to manage containerized applications in different kind of environments such as physical, virtual, and cloud infrastructure. It is an open source system which helps in creating and managing containerization of application. This tutorial provides an overview of different kind of features and functionalities of Kubernetes and teaches how to manage the containerized infrastructure and application deployment.

Audience

This tutorial has been prepared for those who want to understand the containerized infrastructure and deployment of application on containers. This tutorial will help in understanding the concepts of container management using Kubernetes.

Prerequisites

We assume anyone who wants to understand Kubernetes should have an understating of how the Docker works, how the Docker images are created, and how they work as a standalone unit. To reach to an advanced configuration in Kubernetes one should understand basic networking and how the protocol communication works.

OVERVIEW

Kubernetes in an open source container management tool hosted by Cloud Native Computing Foundation (CNCF). This is also known as the enhanced version of Borg which was developed at Google to manage both long running processes and batch jobs, which was earlier handled by separate systems.

Kubernetes comes with a capability of automating deployment, scaling of application, and operations of application containers across clusters. It is capable of creating container centric infrastructure.

Features of Kubernetes

Following are some of the important features of Kubernetes.

- Continues development, integration and deployment
- Containerized infrastructure
- Application-centric management
- Auto-scalable infrastructure
- Environment consistency across development testing and production
- Loosely coupled infrastructure, where each component can act as a separate unit
- Higher density of resource utilization
- Predictable infrastructure which is going to be created

One of the key components of Kubernetes is, it can run application on clusters of physical and virtual machine infrastructure. It also has the capability to run applications on cloud. It helps in moving from host-centric infrastructure to container-centric infrastructure.

ARCHITECTURE

In this chapter, we will discuss the basic architecture of Kubernetes.

Cluster Architecture

As seen in the following diagram, Kubernetes follows client-server architecture. Wherein, we have master installed on one machine and the node on separate Linux machines.

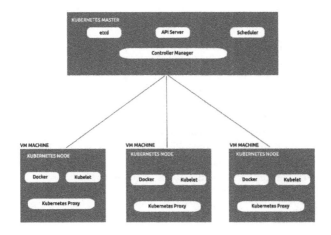

The key components of master and node are defined in the following section.

Master Machine Components

Following are the components of Kubernetes Master Machine.

etcd

It stores the configuration information which can be used by each of the nodes in the cluster. It is a high availability key value store that can be distributed among multiple nodes. It is accessible only by Kubernetes API server as it may have some sensitive information. It is a distributed key value Store which is accessible to all.

API Server

Kubernetes is an API server which provides all the operation on cluster using the API. API server implements an interface, which means different tools and libraries can readily communicate with it. Kubeconfig is a package along with the server side tools that can be used for communication. It exposes Kubernetes API.

Controller Manager

This component is responsible for most of the collectors that regulates the state of cluster and performs a task. In general, it can be considered as a daemon which runs in nonterminating loop and is responsible for collecting and sending information to API server. It works toward getting the shared state of cluster and then make changes to bring the current status of the server to the desired state. The key controllers are replication controller, endpoint controller, namespace controller, and service account controller. The controller manager runs different kind of controllers to handle nodes, endpoints, etc.

Scheduler

This is one of the key components of Kubernetes master. It is a service in master responsible for distributing the workload. It is responsible for tracking utilization of working load on cluster nodes and then placing the workload on which resources are available and accept the workload. In other words, this is the mechanism responsible for allocating pods to available nodes. The scheduler is responsible for workload utilization and allocating pod to new node.

Node Components

Following are the key components of Node server which are necessary to communicate with Kubernetes master.

Docker

The first requirement of each node is Docker which helps in running the encapsulated application containers in a relatively isolated but lightweight operating environment.

Kubelet Service

This is a small service in each node responsible for relaying information to and from control plane service. It interacts with etcd store to read configuration details and wright values. This communicates with the master component to receive commands and work. The kubelet process then assumes responsibility for maintaining the state of work and the node server. It manages network rules, port forwarding, etc.

Kubernetes Proxy Service

This is a proxy service which runs on each node and helps in making services available to the external host. It helps in forwarding the request to correct containers and is capable of performing primitive load balancing. It makes sure that the networking environment is predictable and accessible and at the same time it is isolated as well. It manages pods volumes, secrets, creating new containers' health checkup, etc.

Master and Node Structure

The following illustrations show the structure of Kubernetes Master and Node.

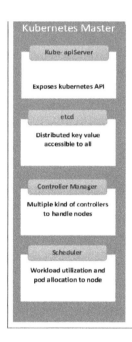

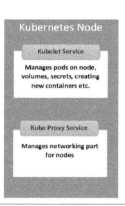

6

SETUP

It is important to set up the Virtual Datacenter (vDC) before setting up Kubernetes. This can be considered as a set of machines where they can communicate with each other via the network. For hands-on approach, you can set up vDC on PROFITBRICKS if you do not have a physical or cloud infrastructure set up.

Once the IaaS setup on any cloud is complete, you need to configure the Master and the Node.

Note − The setup is shown for Ubuntu machines. The same can be set up on other Linux machines as well.

Prerequisites

Installing Docker − Docker is required on all the instances of Kubernetes. Following are the steps to install the Docker.

Step 1 − Log on to the machine with the root user account.

Step 2 − Update the package information. Make sure that the apt package is working.

Step 3 − Run the following commands.

```
$ sudo apt-get update
$ sudo apt-get install apt-transport-https ca-certificates
```

Step 4 − Add the new GPG key.

```
$ sudo apt-key adv \
   --keyserver hkp://ha.pool.sks-keyservers.net:80 \
   --recv-keys 58118E89F3A912897C070ADBF76221572C52609D
$ echo "deb https://apt.dockerproject.org/repo ubuntu-trusty main" | sudo tee
/etc/apt/sources.list.d/docker.list
```

Step 5 − Update the API package image.

```
$ sudo apt-get update
```

Once all the above tasks are complete, you can start with the actual installation of the Docker engine. However, before this you need to verify that the kernel version you are using is correct.

Install Docker Engine

Run the following commands to install the Docker engine.

Step 1 − Logon to the machine.

Step 2 − Update the package index.

```
$ sudo apt-get update
```

Step 3 − Install the Docker Engine using the following command.

```
$ sudo apt-get install docker-engine
```

Step 4 − Start the Docker daemon.

```
$ sudo apt-get install docker-engine
```

Step 5 − To very if the Docker is installed, use the following command.

```
$ sudo docker run hello-world
```

Install etcd 2.0

This needs to be installed on Kubernetes Master Machine. In order to install it, run the following commands.

```
$ curl -L https://github.com/coreos/etcd/releases/download/v2.0.0/etcd
-v2.0.0-linux-amd64.tar.gz -o etcd-v2.0.0-linux-amd64.tar.gz ->1
$ tar xzvf etcd-v2.0.0-linux-amd64.tar.gz ------>2
$ cd etcd-v2.0.0-linux-amd64 ------------>3
$ mkdir /opt/bin ------------->4
$ cp etcd* /opt/bin ----------->5
```

In the above set of command −

- First, we download the etcd. Save this with specified name.
- Then, we have to un-tar the tar package.
- We make a dir. inside the /opt named bin.
- Copy the extracted file to the target location.

Now we are ready to build Kubernetes. We need to install Kubernetes on all the machines on the cluster.

```
$ git clone https://github.com/GoogleCloudPlatform/kubernetes.git
$ cd kubernetes
$ make release
```

The above command will create a _output dir in the root of the kubernetes folder. Next, we can extract the directory into any of the directory of our choice /opt/bin, etc.

Next, comes the networking part wherein we need to actually start with the setup of Kubernetes master and node. In order to do this, we will make an entry in the host file which can be done on the node machine.

```
$ echo "<IP address of master machine> kube-master
< IP address of Node Machine>" >> /etc/hosts
```

Following will be the output of the above command.

```
root@boot2docker:/etc# cat /etc/hosts
127.0.0.1 boot2docker localhost localhost.local

# The following lines are desirable for IPv6 capable hosts
# (added automatically by netbase upgrade)

::1      ip6-localhost ip6-loopback
fe00::0 ip6-localnet
ff00::0 ip6-mcastprefix
ff02::1 ip6-allnodes
ff02::2 ip6-allrouters
ff02::3 ip6-allhosts

10.11.50.12 kube-master
10.11.50.11  kube-minion
```

Now, we will start with the actual configuration on Kubernetes Master.

First, we will start copying all the configuration files to their correct location.

```
$ cp <Current dir. location>/kube-apiserver /opt/bin/
$ cp <Current dir. location>/kube-controller-manager /opt/bin/
$ cp <Current dir. location>/kube-kube-scheduler /opt/bin/
$ cp <Current dir. location>/kubecfg /opt/bin/
$ cp <Current dir. location>/kubectl /opt/bin/
$ cp <Current dir. location>/kubernetes /opt/bin/
```

The above command will copy all the configuration files to the required location. Now we will come back to the same directory where we have built the Kubernetes folder.

```
$ cp kubernetes/cluster/ubuntu/init_conf/kube-apiserver.conf /etc/init/
$ cp kubernetes/cluster/ubuntu/init_conf/kube-controller-manager.conf
/etc/init/
$ cp kubernetes/cluster/ubuntu/init_conf/kube-kube-scheduler.conf
/etc/init/

$ cp kubernetes/cluster/ubuntu/initd_scripts/kube-apiserver /etc/init.d/
$ cp kubernetes/cluster/ubuntu/initd_scripts/kube-controller-manager
/etc/init.d/
$ cp kubernetes/cluster/ubuntu/initd_scripts/kube-kube-scheduler
/etc/init.d/

$ cp kubernetes/cluster/ubuntu/default_scripts/kubelet /etc/default/
$ cp kubernetes/cluster/ubuntu/default_scripts/kube-proxy /etc/default/
$ cp kubernetes/cluster/ubuntu/default_scripts/kubelet /etc/default/
```

The next step is to update the copied configuration file under /etc. dir.

Configure etcd on master using the following command.

```
$ ETCD_OPTS = "-listen-client-urls = http://kube-master:4001"
```

Configure kube-apiserver

For this on the master, we need to edit the /etc/default/kube-apiserver file which we copied earlier.

```
$ KUBE_APISERVER_OPTS = "--address = 0.0.0.0 \
--port = 8080 \
--etcd_servers = <The path that is configured in ETCD_OPTS> \
--portal_net = 11.1.1.0/24 \
--allow_privileged = false \
--kubelet_port = < Port you want to configure> \
--v = 0"
```

Configure the kube Controller Manager

We need to add the following content in /etc/default/kube-controller-manager.

```
$ KUBE_CONTROLLER_MANAGER_OPTS = "--address = 0.0.0.0 \
--master = 127.0.0.1:8080 \
--machines = kube-minion \ -----> #this is the kubernatics node
--v = 0
```

Next, configure the kube scheduler in the corresponding file.

```
$ KUBE_SCHEDULER_OPTS = "--address = 0.0.0.0 \
--master = 127.0.0.1:8080 \
--v = 0"
```

Once all the above tasks are complete, we are good to go ahead by bring up the Kubernetes Master. In order to do this, we will restart the Docker.

```
$ service docker restart
```

Kubernetes Node Configuration

Kubernetes node will run two services the kubelet and the kube-proxy. Before moving ahead, we need to copy the binaries we downloaded to their required folders where we want to configure the kubernetes node.

Use the same method of copying the files that we did for kubernetes master. As it will only run the kubelet and the kube-proxy, we will configure them.

```
$ cp <Path of the extracted file>/kubelet /opt/bin/
$ cp <Path of the extracted file>/kube-proxy /opt/bin/
$ cp <Path of the extracted file>/kubecfg /opt/bin/
$ cp <Path of the extracted file>/kubectl /opt/bin/
$ cp <Path of the extracted file>/kubernetes /opt/bin/
```

Now, we will copy the content to the appropriate dir.

```
$ cp kubernetes/cluster/ubuntu/init_conf/kubelet.conf /etc/init/
$ cp kubernetes/cluster/ubuntu/init_conf/kube-proxy.conf /etc/init/
$ cp kubernetes/cluster/ubuntu/initd_scripts/kubelet /etc/init.d/
$ cp kubernetes/cluster/ubuntu/initd_scripts/kube-proxy /etc/init.d/
$ cp kubernetes/cluster/ubuntu/default_scripts/kubelet /etc/default/
$ cp kubernetes/cluster/ubuntu/default_scripts/kube-proxy /etc/default/
```

We will configure the kubelet and kube-proxy conf files.

We will configure the /etc/init/kubelet.conf.

```
$ KUBELET_OPTS = "--address = 0.0.0.0 \
--port = 10250 \
--hostname_override = kube-minion \
--etcd_servers = http://kube-master:4001 \
--enable_server = true
--v = 0"
/
```

For kube-proxy, we will configure using the following command.

```
$ KUBE_PROXY_OPTS = "--etcd_servers = http://kube-master:4001 \
--v = 0"
/etc/init/kube-proxy.conf
```

12

Finally, we will restart the Docker service.

```
$ service docker restart
```

Now we are done with the configuration. You can check by running the following commands.

```
$ /opt/bin/kubectl get minions
```

IMAGES

Kubernetes (Docker) images are the key building blocks of Containerized Infrastructure. As of now, we are only supporting Kubernetes to support Docker images. Each container in a pod has its Docker image running inside it.

When we are configuring a pod, the image property in the configuration file has the same syntax as the Docker command does. The configuration file has a field to define the image name, which we are planning to pull from the registry.

Following is the common configuration structure which will pull image from Docker registry and deploy in to Kubernetes container.

```
apiVersion: v1
kind: pod
metadata:
   name: Tesing_for_Image_pull -----------> 1
   spec:
     containers:
        - name: neo4j-server -----------------------> 2
        image: <Name of the Docker image>----------> 3
        imagePullPolicy: Always ------------->4
        command: ["echo", "SUCCESS"] -------------------->
```

In the above code, we have defined −

- name: Tesing_for_Image_pull − This name is given to identify and check what is the name of the container that would get created after pulling the images from Docker registry.

- name: neo4j-server − This is the name given to the container that we are trying to create. Like we have given neo4j-server.

- image: <Name of the Docker image> – This is the name of the image which we are trying to pull from the Docker or internal registry of images. We need to define a complete registry path along with the image name that we are trying to pull.

- imagePullPolicy – Always - This image pull policy defines that whenever we run this file to create the container, it will pull the same name again.

- command: ["echo", "SUCCESS"] – With this, when we create the container and if everything goes fine, it will display a message when we will access the container.

In order to pull the image and create a container, we will run the following command.

```
$ kubectl create –f Tesing_for_Image_pull
```

Once we fetch the log, we will get the output as successful.

```
$ kubectl log Tesing_for_Image_pull
```

The above command will produce an output of success or we will get an output as failure.

Note – It is recommended that you try all the commands yourself.

JOBS

The main function of a job is to create one or more pod and tracks about the success of pods. They ensure that the specified number of pods are completed successfully. When a specified number of successful run of pods is completed, then the job is considered complete.

Creating a Job

Use the following command to create a job −

```
apiVersion: v1
kind: Job -----------------------> 1
metadata:
  name: py
  spec:
  template:
    metadata
    name: py -------> 2
    spec:
      containers:
        - name: py -----------------------> 3
        image: python----------> 4
        command: ["python", "SUCCESS"]
        restartPoclıy: Never --------> 5
```

In the above code, we have defined −

- kind: Job → We have defined the kind as Job which will tell kubectl that the yaml file being used is to create a job type pod.

- Name:py → This is the name of the template that we are using and the spec defines the template.

- name: py → we have given a name as py under container spec which helps to identify the Pod which is going to be created out of it.

- Image: python → the image which we are going to pull to create the container which will run inside the pod.

- restartPolicy: Never →This condition of image restart is given as never which means that if the container is killed or if it is false, then it will not restart itself.

We will create the job using the following command with yaml which is saved with the name py.yaml.

```
$ kubectl create –f py.yaml
```

The above command will create a job. If you want to check the status of a job, use the following command.

```
$ kubectl describe jobs/py
```

The above command will create a job. If you want to check the status of a job, use the following command.

Scheduled Job

Scheduled job in Kubernetes uses Cronetes, which takes Kubernetes job and launches them in Kubernetes cluster.

- Scheduling a job will run a pod at a specified point of time.

- A parodic job is created for it which invokes itself automatically.

Note − The feature of a scheduled job is supported by version 1.4 and the betch/v2alpha 1 API is turned on by passing the – runtime-config=batch/v2alpha1 while bringing up the API server.

We will use the same yaml which we used to create the job and make it a scheduled job.

```
apiVersion: v1
kind: Job
```

```
metadata:
  name: py
spec:
  schedule: h/30 * * * ? ------------------> 1
  template:
    metadata
      name: py
    spec:
      containers:
      - name: py
        image: python
        args:
/bin/sh -------> 2
-c
ps -eaf ------------> 3
restartPochy: OnFailure
```

In the above code, we have defined –

- schedule: h/30 * * * ? → To schedule the job to run in
  every 30 minutes.

- /bin/sh: This will enter in the container with /bin/sh

- ps –eaf → Will run ps -eaf command on the machine and
  list all the running process inside a container.

This scheduled job concept is useful when we are trying to build
and run a set of tasks at a specified point of time and then
complete the process.

LABELS & SELECTORS

Labels

Labels are key-value pairs which are attached to pods, replication controller and services. They are used as identifying attributes for objects such as pods and replication controller. They can be added to an object at creation time and can be added or modified at the run time.

Selectors

Labels do not provide uniqueness. In general, we can say many objects can carry the same labels. Labels selector are core grouping primitive in Kubernetes. They are used by the users to select a set of objects.

Kubernetes API currently supports two type of selectors −

- Equality-based selectors
- Set-based selectors
- Equality-based Selectors

They allow filtering by key and value. Matching objects should satisfy all the specified labels.

Set-based Selectors

Set-based selectors allow filtering of keys according to a set of values.

```
apiVersion: v1
kind: Service
metadata:
```

```
    name: sp-neo4j-standalone
spec:
  ports:
    - port: 7474
    name: neo4j
  type: NodePort
  selector:
    app: salesplatform ---------> 1
    component: neo4j -----------> 2
```

In the above code, we are using the label selector as app: salesplatform and component as component: neo4j.

Once we run the file using the kubectl command, it will create a service with the name sp-neo4j-standalone which will communicate on port 7474. The ype is NodePort with the new label selector as app: salesplatform and component: neo4j.

NAMESPACE

Namespace provides an additional qualification to a resource name. This is helpful when multiple teams are using the same cluster and there is a potential of name collision. It can be as a virtual wall between multiple clusters.

Functionality of Namespace

Following are some of the important functionalities of a Namespace in Kubernetes −

- Namespaces help pod-to-pod communication using the same namespace.

- Namespaces are virtual clusters that can sit on top of the same physical cluster.

- They provide logical separation between the teams and their environments.

Create a Namespace

The following command is used to create a namespace.

```
apiVersion: v1
kind: Namespce
metadata
  name: elk
```

Control the Namespace

The following command is used to control the namespace.

```
$ kubectl create –f namespace.yml ---------> 1
$ kubectl get namespace -----------------> 2
$ kubectl get namespace <Namespace name> ------->3
$ kubectl describe namespace <Namespace name> ---->4
$ kubectl delete namespace <Namespace name>
```

In the above code,

- We are using the command to create a namespace.

- This will list all the available namespace.

- This will get a particular namespace whose name is specified in the command.

- This will describe the complete details about the service.

- This will delete a particular namespace present in the cluster.

Using Namespace in Service - Example

Following is an example of a sample file for using namespace in service.

```
apiVersion: v1
kind: Service
metadata:
  name: elasticsearch
  namespace: elk
  labels:
    component: elasticsearch
spec:
  type: LoadBalancer
  selector:
    component: elasticsearch
  ports:
  - name: http
    port: 9200
    protocol: TCP
  - name: transport
    port: 9300
    protocol: TCP
```

In the above code, we are using the same namespace under service metadata with the name of elk.

NODE

A node is a working machine in Kubernetes cluster which is also known as a minion. They are working units which can be physical, VM, or a cloud instance.

Each node has all the required configuration required to run a pod on it such as the proxy service and kubelet service along with the Docker, which is used to run the Docker containers on the pod created on the node.

They are not created by Kubernetes but they are created externally either by the cloud service provider or the Kubernetes cluster manager on physical or VM machines.

The key component of Kubernetes to handle multiple nodes is the controller manager, which runs multiple kind of controllers to manage nodes. To manage nodes, Kubernetes creates an object of kind node which will validate that the object which is created is a valid node.

Service with Selector

```
apiVersion: v1
kind: node
metadata:
  name: < ip address of the node>
  labels:
    name: <lable name>
```

In JSON format the actual object is created which looks as follows −

```
{
  Kind: node
  apiVersion: v1
  "metadata":
  {
    "name": "10.01.1.10",
    "labels"
    {
      "name": "cluster 1 node"
    }
```

```
  }
}
```

Node Controller

They are the collection of services which run in the Kubernetes master and continuously monitor the node in the cluster on the basis of metadata.name. If all the required services are running, then the node is validated and a newly created pod will be assigned to that node by the controller. If it is not valid, then the master will not assign any pod to it and will wait until it becomes valid.

Kubernetes master registers the node automatically, if –register-node flag is true.

```
–register-node = true
```

However, if the cluster administrator wants to manage it manually then it could be done by turning the flat of –

```
–register-node = false
```

SERVICE

A service can be defined as a logical set of pods. It can be defined as an abstraction on the top of the pod which provides a single IP address and DNS name by which pods can be accessed. With Service, it is very easy to manage load balancing configuration. It helps pods to scale very easily.

A service is a REST object in Kubernetes whose definition can be posted to Kubernetes apiServer on the Kubernetes master to create a new instance.

Service without Selector

```
apiVersion: v1
kind: Service
metadata:
  name: Tutorial_point_service
spec:
  ports:
  - port: 8080
  targetPort: 31999
```

The above configuration will create a service with the name Tutorial_point_service.

Service Config File with Selector

```
apiVersion: v1
kind: Service
metadata:
  name: Tutorial_point_service
spec:
  selector:
    application: "My Application" -------------------> (Selector)
  ports:
  - port: 8080
  targetPort: 31999
```

In this example, we have a selector; so in order to transfer traffic, we need to create an endpoint manually.

```
apiVersion: v1
kind: Endpoints
metadata:
  name: Tutorial_point_service
subnets:
  address:
    "ip": "192.168.168.40" ------------------> (Selector)
  ports:
    - port: 8080
```

In the above code, we have created an endpoint which will route the traffic to the endpoint defined as "192.168.168.40:8080".

Multi-Port Service Creation

```
apiVersion: v1
kind: Service
metadata:
  name: Tutorial_point_service
spec:
  selector:
    application: "My Application" ------------------> (Selector)
  ClusterIP: 10.3.0.12
  ports:
    -name: http
    protocol: TCP
    port: 80
    targetPort: 31999
   -name:https
    Protocol: TCP
    Port: 443
    targetPort: 31998
```

Types of Services

ClusterIP − This helps in restricting the service within the cluster. It exposes the service within the defined Kubernetes cluster.

```
spec:
  type: NodePort
```

```
ports:
- port: 8080
  nodePort: 31999
  name: NodeportService
```

NodePort — It will expose the service on a static port on the deployed node. A ClusterIP service, to which NodePort service will route, is automatically created. The service can be accessed from outside the cluster using the NodeIP:nodePort.

```
spec:
  ports:
  - port: 8080
    nodePort: 31999
    name: NodeportService
    clusterIP: 10.20.30.40
```

Load Balancer — It uses cloud providers' load balancer. NodePort and ClusterIP services are created automatically to which the external load balancer will route.

A full service yaml file with service type as Node Port. Try to create one yourself.

```
apiVersion: v1
kind: Service
metadata:
  name: appname
  labels:
    k8s-app: appname
spec:
  type: NodePort
  ports:
  - port: 8080
    nodePort: 31999
    name: omninginx
  selector:
    k8s-app: appname
    component: nginx
    env: env_name
```

POD

A pod is a collection of containers and its storage inside a node of a Kubernetes cluster. It is possible to create a pod with multiple containers inside it. For example, keeping a database container and data container in the same pod.

Types of Pod

There are two types of Pods −

- Single container pod
- Multi container pod

Single Container Pod

They can be simply created with the kubctl run command, where you have a defined image on the Docker registry which we will pull while creating a pod.

```
$ kubectl run <name of pod> --image=<name of the image from registry>
```

Example − We will create a pod with a tomcat image which is available on the Docker hub.

```
$ kubectl run tomcat --image = tomcat:8.0
```

This can also be done by creating the yaml file and then running the kubectl create command.

```
apiVersion: v1
kind: Pod
metadata:
  name: Tomcat
spec:
  containers:
  - name: Tomcat
   image: tomcat: 8.0
   ports:
containerPort: 7500
```

```
imagePullPolicy: Always
```

Once the above yaml file is created, we will save the file with the
name of tomcat.yml and run the create command to run the
document.

```
$ kubectl create –f tomcat.yml
```

It will create a pod with the name of tomcat. We can use the
describe command along with kubectl to describe the pod.

Multi Container Pod

Multi container pods are created using yaml mail with the
definition of the containers.

```
apiVersion: v1
kind: Pod
metadata:
  name: Tomcat
spec:
  containers:
  - name: Tomcat
   image: tomcat: 8.0
   ports:
containerPort: 7500
   imagePullPolicy: Always
   -name: Database
   Image: mongoDB
   Ports:
containerPort: 7501
   imagePullPolicy: Always
```

In the above code, we have created one pod with two containers
inside it, one for tomcat and the other for MongoDB.

REPLICATION CONTROLLER

Replication Controller is one of the key features of Kubernetes, which is responsible for managing the pod lifecycle. It is responsible for making sure that the specified number of pod replicas are running at any point of time. It is used in time when one wants to make sure that the specified number of pod or at least one pod is running. It has the capability to bring up or down the specified no of pod.

It is a best practice to use the replication controller to manage the pod life cycle rather than creating a pod again and again.

```
apiVersion: v1
kind: ReplicationController -------------------------> 1
metadata:
   name: Tomcat-ReplicationController -------------------------> 2
spec:
   replicas: 3 -----------------------> 3
   template:
      metadata:
         name: Tomcat-ReplicationController
      labels:
         app: App
         component: neo4j
      spec:
         containers:
         - name: Tomcat- -----------------------> 4
         image: tomcat: 8.0
         ports:
            - containerPort: 7474 -----------------------> 5
```

Setup Details

- Kind: ReplicationController → In the above code, we have defined the kind as replication controller which tells the kubectl that the yaml file is going to be used for creating the replication controller.

- name: Tomcat-ReplicationController → This helps in identifying the name with which the replication controller will be created. If we run the kubctl, get rc < Tomcat-ReplicationController > it will show the replication controller details.

- replicas: 3 → This helps the replication controller to understand that it needs to maintain three replicas of a pod at any point of time in the pod lifecycle.

- name: Tomcat → In the spec section, we have defined the name as tomcat which will tell the replication controller that the container present inside the pods is tomcat.

- containerPort: 7474 → It helps in making sure that all the nodes in the cluster where the pod is running the container inside the pod will be exposed on the same port 7474.

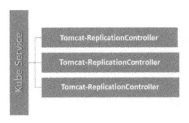

Here, the Kubernetes service is working as a load balancer for three tomcat replicas.

REPLICA SETS

Replica Set ensures how many replica of pod should be running. It can be considered as a replacement of replication controller. The key difference between the replica set and the replication controller is, the replication controller only supports equality-based selector whereas the replica set supports set-based selector.

```
apiVersion: extensions/v1beta1 -------------------->1
kind: ReplicaSet ------------------------> 2
metadata:
  name: Tomcat-ReplicaSet
spec:
  replicas: 3
  selector:
    matchLables:
      tier: Backend -----------------> 3
    matchExpression:
{ key: tier, operation: In, values: [Backend]} -------------> 4
template:
  metadata:
    lables:
      app: Tomcat-ReplicaSet
      tier: Backend
    labels:
      app: App
      component: neo4j
  spec:
    containers:
    - name: Tomcat
    image: tomcat: 8.0
    ports:
    - containerPort: 7474
```

Setup Details

- apiVersion: extensions/v1beta1 → In the above code, the API version is the advanced beta version of Kubernetes which supports the concept of replica set.

- kind: ReplicaSet → We have defined the kind as the replica set which helps kubectl to understand that the file is used to create a replica set.

- tier: Backend → We have defined the label tier as backend which creates a matching selector.

- {key: tier, operation: In, values: [Backend]} → This will help matchExpression to understand the matching condition we have defined and in the operation which is used by matchlabel to find details.

Run the above file using kubectl and create the backend replica set with the provided definition in the yaml file.

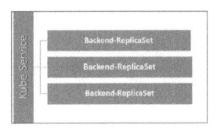

DEPLOYMENTS

Deployments are upgraded and higher version of replication controller. They manage the deployment of replica sets which is also an upgraded version of the replication controller. They have the capability to update the replica set and are also capable of rolling back to the previous version.

They provide many updated features of matchLabels and selectors. We have got a new controller in the Kubernetes master called the deployment controller which makes it happen. It has the capability to change the deployment midway.

Changing the Deployment

Updating − The user can update the ongoing deployment before it is completed. In this, the existing deployment will be settled and new deployment will be created.

Deleting − The user can pause/cancel the deployment by deleting it before it is completed. Recreating the same deployment will resume it.

Rollback − We can roll back the deployment or the deployment in progress. The user can create or update the deployment by using DeploymentSpec.PodTemplateSpec = oldRC.PodTemplateSpec.

Deployment Strategies

Deployment strategies help in defining how the new RC should replace the existing RC.

Recreate − This feature will kill all the existing RC and then bring up the new ones. This results in quick deployment however it will result in downtime when the old pods are down and the new pods have not come up.

Rolling Update − This feature gradually brings down the old RC and brings up the new one. This results in slow deployment, however there is no deployment. At all times, few old pods and few new pods are available in this process.

The configuration file of Deployment looks like this.

```
apiVersion: extensions/v1beta1 -------------------->1
kind: Deployment -------------------------> 2
metadata:
  name: Tomcat-ReplicaSet
spec:
  replicas: 3
  template:
    metadata:
      lables:
        app: Tomcat-ReplicaSet
        tier: Backend
    spec:
      containers:
        - name: Tomcatimage:
          tomcat: 8.0
          ports:
            - containerPort: 7474
```

In the above code, the only thing which is different from the replica set is we have defined the kind as deployment.

Create Deployment

```
$ kubectl create –f Deployment.yaml --record
deployment "Deployment" created Successfully.
```

Fetch the Deployment

```
$ kubectl get deployments
NAME        DESIRED   CURRENT   UP-TO-DATE   AVILABLE
AGE
Deployment   3        3         3            3    20s
```

Check the Status of Deployment

```
$ kubectl rollout status deployment/Deployment
```

Updating the Deployment

```
$ kubectl set image deployment/Deployment tomcat=tomcat:6.0
```

Rolling Back to Previous Deployment

```
$ kubectl rollout undo deployment/Deployment --to-revision=2
```

VOLUMES

In Kubernetes, a volume can be thought of as a directory which is accessible to the containers in a pod. We have different types of volumes in Kubernetes and the type defines how the volume is created and its content.

The concept of volume was present with the Docker, however the only issue was that the volume was very much limited to a particular pod. As soon as the life of a pod ended, the volume was also lost.

On the other hand, the volumes that are created through Kubernetes is not limited to any container. It supports any or all the containers deployed inside the pod of Kubernetes. A key advantage of Kubernetes volume is, it supports different kind of storage wherein the pod can use multiple of them at the same time.

Types of Kubernetes Volume

Here is a list of some popular Kubernetes Volumes −

- emptyDir − It is a type of volume that is created when a Pod is first assigned to a Node. It remains active as long as the Pod is running on that node. The volume is initially empty and the containers in the pod can read and write the files in the emptyDir volume. Once the Pod is removed from the node, the data in the emptyDir is erased.

- hostPath − This type of volume mounts a file or directory from the host node's filesystem into your pod.

- gcePersistentDisk − This type of volume mounts a Google Compute Engine (GCE) Persistent Disk into your Pod. The data in a gcePersistentDisk remains intact when the Pod is removed from the node.

- awsElasticBlockStore – This type of volume mounts an Amazon Web Services (AWS) Elastic Block Store into your Pod. Just like gcePersistentDisk, the data in an awsElasticBlockStore remains intact when the Pod is removed from the node.

- nfs – An nfs volume allows an existing NFS (Network File System) to be mounted into your pod. The data in an nfs volume is not erased when the Pod is removed from the node. The volume is only unmounted.

- iscsi – An iscsi volume allows an existing iSCSI (SCSI over IP) volume to be mounted into your pod.

- flocker – It is an open-source clustered container data volume manager. It is used for managing data volumes. A flocker volume allows a Flocker dataset to be mounted into a pod. If the dataset does not exist in Flocker, then you first need to create it by using the Flocker API.

- glusterfs – Glusterfs is an open-source networked filesystem. A glusterfs volume allows a glusterfs volume to be mounted into your pod.

- rbd – RBD stands for Rados Block Device. An rbd volume allows a Rados Block Device volume to be mounted into your pod. Data remains preserved after the Pod is removed from the node.

- cephfs – A cephfs volume allows an existing CephFS volume to be mounted into your pod. Data remains intact after the Pod is removed from the node.

- gitRepo – A gitRepo volume mounts an empty directory and clones a git repository into it for your pod to use.

- secret – A secret volume is used to pass sensitive information, such as passwords, to pods.

- persistentVolumeClaim —
A persistentVolumeClaim volume is used to mount a
PersistentVolume into a pod. PersistentVolumes are a way
for users to "claim" durable storage (such as a GCE
PersistentDisk or an iSCSI volume) without knowing the
details of the particular cloud environment.

- downwardAPI — A downwardAPI volume is used to make
downward API data available to applications. It mounts a
directory and writes the requested data in plain text files.

- azureDiskVolume — An AzureDiskVolume is used to
mount a Microsoft Azure Data Disk into a Pod.

Persistent Volume and Persistent Volume Claim

Persistent Volume (PV) — It's a piece of network storage that
has been provisioned by the administrator. It's a resource in the
cluster which is independent of any individual pod that uses the
PV.

Persistent Volume Claim (PVC) — The storage requested by
Kubernetes for its pods is known as PVC. The user does not
need to know the underlying provisioning. The claims must be
created in the same namespace where the pod is created.

Creating Persistent Volume

```
kind: PersistentVolume --------> 1
apiVersion: v1
metadata:
  name: pv0001 ----------------> 2
  labels:
    type: local
spec:
  capacity: ---------------------> 3
    storage: 10Gi ---------------> 4
  accessModes:
    - ReadWriteOnce -------------> 5
    hostPath:
      path: "/tmp/data01" -------------------------> 6
```

In the above code, we have defined −

- kind: PersistentVolume → We have defined the kind as PersistentVolume which tells kubernetes that the yaml file being used is to create the Persistent Volume.

- name: pv0001 → Name of PersistentVolume that we are creating.

- capacity: → This spec will define the capacity of PV that we are trying to create.

- storage: 10Gi → This tells the underlying infrastructure that we are trying to claim 10Gi space on the defined path.

- ReadWriteOnce → This tells the access rights of the volume that we are creating.

- path: "/tmp/data01" → This definition tells the machine that we are trying to create volume under this path on the underlying infrastructure.

Creating PV

```
$ kubectl create –f local-01.yaml
persistentvolume "pv0001" created
```

Checking PV

```
$ kubectl get pv
NAME      CAPACITY    ACCESSMODES    STATUS    CLAIM
REASON    AGE
pv0001    10Gi        RWO            Available           14s
```

Describing PV

```
$ kubectl describe pv pv0001
```

Creating Persistent Volume Claim

```
kind: PersistentVolumeClaim --------------> 1
apiVersion: v1
metadata:
  name: myclaim-1 --------------------> 2
spec:
  accessModes:
    - ReadWriteOnce ------------------------> 3
  resources:
    requests:
      storage: 3Gi ---------------------> 4
```

In the above code, we have defined −

- kind: PersistentVolumeClaim → It instructs the underlying infrastructure that we are trying to claim a specified amount of space.

- name: myclaim-1 → Name of the claim that we are trying to create.

- ReadWriteOnce → This specifies the mode of the claim that we are trying to create.

- storage: 3Gi → This will tell kubernetes about the amount of space we are trying to claim.

Creating PVC

```
$ kubectl create –f myclaim-1
persistentvolumeclaim "myclaim-1" created
```

Getting Details About PVC

```
$ kubectl get pvc
NAME        STATUS  VOLUME  CAPACITY  ACCESSMODES  AGE
myclaim-1   Bound   pv0001  10Gi      RWO          7s
```

Describe PVC

```
$ kubectl describe pv pv0001
```

Using PV and PVC with POD

```
kind: Pod
apiVersion: v1
metadata:
  name: mypod
  labels:
    name: frontendhttp
spec:
  containers:
  - name: myfrontend
    image: nginx
    ports:
    - containerPort: 80
      name: "http-server"
    volumeMounts: ----------------------------> 1
    - mountPath: "/usr/share/tomcat/html"
      name: mypd
  volumes: ----------------------> 2
    - name: mypd
      persistentVolumeClaim: ------------------------>3
      claimName: myclaim-1
```

In the above code, we have defined −

- volumeMounts: → This is the path in the container on which the mounting will take place.

- Volume: → This definition defines the volume definition that we are going to claim.

- persistentVolumeClaim: → Under this, we define the volume name which we are going to use in the defined pod.

SECRETS

Secrets can be defined as Kubernetes objects used to store sensitive data such as user name and passwords with encryption.

There are multiple ways of creating secrets in Kubernetes.

- Creating from txt files.
- Creating from yaml file.

Creating From Text File

In order to create secrets from a text file such as user name and password, we first need to store them in a txt file and use the following command.

```
$ kubectl create secret generic tomcat-passwd —from-file = ./username.txt —
fromfile = ./.
password.txt
```

Creating From Yaml File

```
apiVersion: v1
kind: Secret
metadata:
name: tomcat-pass
type: Opaque
data:
  password: <User Password>
  username: <User Name>
```

Creating the Secret

```
$ kubectl create –f Secret.yaml
secrets/tomcat-pass
```

Using Secrets

Once we have created the secrets, it can be consumed in a pod or the replication controller as −

- Environment Variable
- Volume

As Environment Variable

In order to use the secret as environment variable, we will use env under the spec section of pod yaml file.

```
env:
- name: SECRET_USERNAME
  valueFrom:
    secretKeyRef:
      name: mysecret
      key: tomcat-pass
```

As Volume

```
spec:
  volumes:
    - name: "secretstest"
      secret:
        secretName: tomcat-pass
  containers:
    - image: tomcat:7.0
      name: awebserver
      volumeMounts:
        - mountPath: "/tmp/mysec"
          name: "secretstest"
```

Secret Configuration As Environment Variable

```
apiVersion: v1
kind: ReplicationController
metadata:
  name: appname
spec:
replicas: replica_count
template:
```

```
metadata:
  name: appname
spec:
  nodeSelector:
    resource-group:
  containers:
    - name: appname
      image:
      imagePullPolicy: Always
      ports:
      - containerPort: 3000
      env: ----------------------------> 1
        - name: ENV
          valueFrom:
            configMapKeyRef:
              name: appname
              key: tomcat-secrets
```

In the above code, under the env definition, we are using secrets as environment variable in the replication controller.

Secrets As Volume Mount

```
apiVersion: v1
kind: pod
metadata:
  name: appname
spec:
  metadata:
    name: appname
  spec:
  volumes:
    - name: "secretstest"
      secret:
        secretName: tomcat-pass
  containers:
    - image: tomcat: 8.0
      name: awebserver
      volumeMounts:
        - mountPath: "/tmp/mysec"
          name: "secretstest"
```

NETWORK POLICY

Network Policy defines how the pods in the same namespace will communicate with each other and the network endpoint. It requires extensions/v1beta1/networkpolicies to be enabled in the runtime configuration in the API server. Its resources use labels to select the pods and define rules to allow traffic to a specific pod in addition to which is defined in the namespace.

First, we need to configure Namespace Isolation Policy. Basically, this kind of networking policies are required on the load balancers.

```
kind: Namespace
apiVersion: v1
metadata:
  annotations:
    net.beta.kubernetes.io/network-policy: |
    {
      "ingress":
      {
        "isolation": "DefaultDeny"
      }
    }
$ kubectl annotate ns <namespace> "net.beta.kubernetes.io/network-policy
=
{\"ingress\": {\"isolation\": \"DefaultDeny\"}}"
```

Once the namespace is created, we need to create the Network Policy.

Network Policy Yaml

```
kind: NetworkPolicy
apiVersion: extensions/v1beta1
metadata:
  name: allow-frontend
  namespace: myns
spec:
  podSelector:
    matchLabels:
      role: backend
  ingress:
```

```yaml
  - from:
    - podSelector:
      matchLabels:
        role: frontend
  ports:
    - protocol: TCP
      port: 6379
```

API

Kubernetes API serves as a foundation for declarative configuration schema for the system. Kubectl command-line tool can be used to create, update, delete, and get API object. Kubernetes API acts a communicator among different components of Kubernetes.

Adding API to Kubernetes

Adding a new API to Kubernetes will add new features to Kubernetes, which will increase the functionality of Kubernetes. However, alongside it will also increase the cost and maintainability of the system. In order to create a balance between the cost and complexity, there are a few sets defined for it.

The API which is getting added should be useful to more than 50% of the users. There is no other way to implement the functionality in Kubernetes. Exceptional circumstances are discussed in the community meeting of Kubernetes, and then API is added.

API Changes

In order to increase the capability of Kubernetes, changes are continuously introduced to the system. It is done by Kubernetes team to add the functionality to Kubernetes without removing or impacting the existing functionality of the system.

To demonstrate the general process, here is an (hypothetical) example −

- A user POSTs a Pod object to /api/v7beta1/...
- The JSON is unmarshalled into a v7beta1.Pod structure
- Default values are applied to the v7beta1.Pod
- The v7beta1.Pod is converted to an api.Pod structure

- The api.Pod is validated, and any errors are returned to the user

- The api.Pod is converted to a v6.Pod (because v6 is the latest stable version)

- The v6.Pod is marshalled into JSON and written to etcd

Now that we have the Pod object stored, a user can GET that object in any supported API version. For example –

- A user GETs the Pod from /api/v5/...

- The JSON is read from etcd and unmarshalled into a v6.Pod structure

- Default values are applied to the v6.Pod

- The v6.Pod is converted to an api.Pod structure

- The api.Pod is converted to a v5.Pod structure

- The v5.Pod is marshalled into JSON and sent to the user

The implication of this process is that API changes must be done carefully and backward compatibly.

API Versioning

To make it easier to support multiple structures, Kubernetes supports multiple API versions each at different API path such as /api/v1 or /apis/extensions/v1beta1

Versioning standards at Kubernetes are defined in multiple standards.

Alpha Level

- This version contains alpha (e.g. v1alpha1)
- This version may be buggy; the enabled version may have bugs
- Support for bugs can be dropped at any point of time.
- Recommended to be used in short term testing only as the support may not be present all the time.

Beta Level

- The version name contains beta (e.g. v2beta3)

- The code is fully tested and the enabled version is supposed to be stable.

- The support of the feature will not be dropped; there may be some small changes.

- Recommended for only non-business-critical uses because of the potential for incompatible changes in subsequent releases.

Stable Level

- The version name is vX where X is an integer.
- Stable versions of features will appear in the released software for many subsequent versions.

KUBECTL

Kubectl is the command line utility to interact with Kubernetes API. It is an interface which is used to communicate and manage pods in Kubernetes cluster.

One needs to set up kubectl to local in order to interact with Kubernetes cluster.

Setting Kubectl

Download the executable to the local workstation using the curl command.

On Linux

```
$ curl -O https://storage.googleapis.com/kubernetesrelease/
release/v1.5.2/bin/linux/amd64/kubectl
```

On OS X workstation

```
$ curl -O https://storage.googleapis.com/kubernetesrelease/
release/v1.5.2/bin/darwin/amd64/kubectl
```

After download is complete, move the binaries in the path of the system.

```
$ chmod +x kubectl
$ mv kubectl /usr/local/bin/kubectl
```

Configuring Kubectl

Following are the steps to perform the configuration operation.

```
$ kubectl config set-cluster default-cluster --server =
https://${MASTER_HOST} --
certificate-authority = ${CA_CERT}

$ kubectl config set-credentials default-admin --certificateauthority = ${
CA_CERT} --client-key = ${ADMIN_KEY} --clientcertificate = ${
```

```
ADMIN_CERT}

$ kubectl config set-context default-system --cluster = default-cluster --
user = default-admin
$ kubectl config use-context default-system
```

- Replace ${MASTER_HOST} with the master node address or name used in the previous steps.

- Replace ${CA_CERT} with the absolute path to the ca.pem created in the previous steps.

- Replace ${ADMIN_KEY} with the absolute path to the admin-key.pem created in the previous steps.

- Replace ${ADMIN_CERT} with the absolute path to the admin.pem created in the previous steps.

Verifying the Setup

To verify if the kubectl is working fine or not, check if the Kubernetes client is set up correctly.

```
$ kubectl get nodes

NAME      LABELS                               STATUS
Vipin.com Kubernetes.io/hostname = vipin.mishra.com   Ready
```

KUBECTL COMMANDS

Kubectl controls the Kubernetes Cluster. It is one of the key components of Kubernetes which runs on the workstation on any machine when the setup is done. It has the capability to manage the nodes in the cluster.

Kubectl commands are used to interact and manage Kubernetes objects and the cluster. In this chapter, we will discuss a few commands used in Kubernetes via kubectl.

kubectl annotate — It updates the annotation on a resource.

```
$kubectl annotate [--overwrite] (-f FILENAME | TYPE NAME)
KEY_1=VAL_1 ...
KEY_N = VAL_N [--resource-version = version]
```

For example,

```
kubectl annotate pods tomcat description = 'my frontend'
```

kubectl api-versions — It prints the supported versions of API on the cluster.

```
$ kubectl api-version;
```

kubectl apply — It has the capability to configure a resource by file or stdin.

```
$ kubectl apply –f <filename>
```

kubectl attach — This attaches things to the running container.

```
$ kubectl attach <pod> –c <container>
$ kubectl attach 123456-7890 -c tomcat-conatiner
```

kubectl autoscale − This is used to auto scale pods which are defined such as Deployment, replica set, Replication Controller.

```
$ kubectl autoscale (-f FILENAME | TYPE NAME | TYPE/NAME) [--
min = MINPODS] --
max = MAXPODS [--cpu-percent = CPU] [flags]
$ kubectl autoscale deployment foo --min = 2 --max = 10
```

kubectl cluster-info − It displays the cluster Info.

```
$ kubectl cluster-info
```

kubectl cluster-info dump − It dumps relevant information regarding cluster for debugging and diagnosis.

```
$ kubectl cluster-info dump
$ kubectl cluster-info dump --output-directory = /path/to/cluster-state
```

kubectl config − Modifies the kubeconfig file.

```
$ kubectl config <SUBCOMMAD>
$ kubectl config --kubeconfig <String of File name>
```

kubectl config current-context − It displays the current context.

```
$ kubectl config current-context
#deploys the current context
```

kubectl config delete-cluster − Deletes the specified cluster from kubeconfig.

```
$ kubectl config delete-cluster <Cluster Name>
```

kubectl config delete-context − Deletes a specified context from kubeconfig.

```
$ kubectl config delete-context <Context Name>
```

kubectl config get-clusters — Displays cluster defined in the kubeconfig.

```
$ kubectl config get-cluster
$ kubectl config get-cluster <Cluser Name>
```

kubectl config get-contexts — Describes one or many contexts.

```
$ kubectl config get-context <Context Name>
```

kubectl config set-cluster — Sets the cluster entry in Kubernetes.

```
$ kubectl config set-cluster NAME [--server = server] [--certificateauthority =
path/to/certificate/authority] [--insecure-skip-tls-verify = true]
```

kubectl config set-context — Sets a context entry in kubernetes entrypoint.

```
$ kubectl config set-context NAME [--cluster = cluster_nickname] [--
user = user_nickname] [--namespace = namespace]
$ kubectl config set-context prod –user = vipin-mishra
```

kubectl config set-credentials — Sets a user entry in kubeconfig.

```
$ kubectl config set-credentials cluster-admin --username = vipin --
password = uXFGweU9l35qcif
```

kubectl config set — Sets an individual value in kubeconfig file.

```
$ kubectl config set PROPERTY_NAME PROPERTY_VALUE
```

kubectl config unset — It unsets a specific component in kubectl.

```
$ kubectl config unset PROPERTY_NAME PROPERTY_VALUE
```

kubectl config use-context – Sets the current context in kubectl file.

```
$ kubectl config use-context <Context Name>
```

kubectl config view

```
$ kubectl config view
$ kubectl config view –o jsonpath='{.users[?(@.name ==
"e2e")].user.password}'
```

kubectl cp – Copy files and directories to and from containers.

```
$ kubectl cp <Files from source> <Files to Destination>
$ kubectl cp /tmp/foo <some-pod>:/tmp/bar -c <specific-container>
```

kubectl create – To create resource by filename of or stdin. To do this, JSON or YAML formats are accepted.

```
$ kubectl create –f <File Name>
$ cat <file name> | kubectl create –f -
```

In the same way, we can create multiple things as listed using the create command along with kubectl.

- deployment
- namespace
- quota
- secret docker-registry
- secret
- secret generic
- secret tls
- serviceaccount
- service clusterip
- service loadbalancer
- service nodeport

kubectl delete – Deletes resources by file name, stdin, resource and names.

```
$ kubectl delete –f ([-f FILENAME] | TYPE [(NAME | -l label | --all)])
```

kubectl describe – Describes any particular resource in kubernetes. Shows details of resource or a group of resources.

```
$ kubectl describe <type> <type name>
$ kubectl describe pod tomcat
```

kubectl drain – This is used to drain a node for maintenance purpose. It prepares the node for maintenance. This will mark the node as unavailable so that it should not be assigned with a new container which will be created.

```
$ kubectl drain tomcat –force
```

kubectl edit − It is used to end the resources on the server. This allows to directly edit a resource which one can receive via the command line tool.

```
$ kubectl edit <Resource/Name | File Name)
Ex.
$ kubectl edit rc/tomcat
```

kubectl exec − This helps to execute a command in the container.

```
$ kubectl exec POD <-c CONTAINER > -- COMMAND < args...>
$ kubectl exec tomcat 123-5-456 date
```

kubectl expose − This is used to expose the Kubernetes objects such as pod, replication controller, and service as a new Kubernetes service. This has the capability to expose it via a running container or from a yaml file.

```
$ kubectl expose (-f FILENAME | TYPE NAME) [--port=port] [--protocol
= TCP|UDP]
[--target-port = number-or-name] [--name = name] [--external-ip = external-
ip-ofservice]
[--type = type]
$ kubectl expose rc tomcat —port=80 –target-port = 30000
$ kubectl expose –f tomcat.yaml –port = 80 –target-port =
```

kubectl get − This command is capable of fetching data on the cluster about the Kubernetes resources.

```
$ kubectl get [(-o|--output=)json|yaml|wide|custom-columns=...|custom-
columnsfile=...|
go-template=...|go-template-file=...|jsonpath=...|jsonpath-file=...]
(TYPE [NAME | -l label] | TYPE/NAME ...) [flags]
```

For example,

```
$ kubectl get pod <pod name>
$ kubectl get service <Service name>
```

kubectl logs – They are used to get the logs of the container in a pod. Printing the logs can be defining the container name in the pod. If the POD has only one container there is no need to define its name.

```
$ kubectl logs [-f] [-p] POD [-c CONTAINER]
Example
$ kubectl logs tomcat.
$ kubectl logs –p –c tomcat.8
```

kubectl port-forward – They are used to forward one or more local port to pods.

```
$ kubectl port-forward POD [LOCAL_PORT:]REMOTE_PORT
[...[LOCAL_PORT_N:]REMOTE_PORT_N]
$ kubectl port-forward tomcat 3000 4000
$ kubectl port-forward tomcat 3000:5000
```

kubectl replace – Capable of replacing a resource by file name or stdin.

```
$ kubectl replace -f FILENAME
$ kubectl replace –f tomcat.yml
$ cat tomcat.yml | kubectl replace –f -
```

kubectl rolling-update – Performs a rolling update on a replication controller. Replaces the specified replication controller with a new replication controller by updating a POD at a time.

```
$ kubectl rolling-update OLD_CONTROLLER_NAME
([NEW_CONTROLLER_NAME] --
image = NEW_CONTAINER_IMAGE | -f
NEW_CONTROLLER_SPEC)
$ kubectl rolling-update frontend-v1 –f freontend-v2.yaml
```

kubectl rollout – It is capable of managing the rollout of deployment.

```
$ Kubectl rollout <Sub Command>
$ kubectl rollout undo deployment/tomcat
```

Apart from the above, we can perform multiple tasks using the rollout such as −

- rollout history
- rollout pause
- rollout resume
- rollout status
- rollout undo

kubectl run − Run command has the capability to run an image on the Kubernetes cluster.

```
$ kubectl run NAME --image = image [--env = "key = value"] [--port = port]
[--
replicas = replicas] [--dry-run = bool] [--overrides = inline-json] [--command]
--
[COMMAND] [args...]
$ kubectl run tomcat --image = tomcat:7.0
$ kubectl run tomcat —image = tomcat:7.0 –port = 5000
```

kubectl scale − It will scale the size of Kubernetes Deployments, ReplicaSet, Replication Controller, or job.

```
$ kubectl scale [--resource-version = version] [--current-replicas = count] --
replicas = COUNT (-f FILENAME | TYPE NAME )
$ kubectl scale —replica = 3 rs/tomcat
$ kubectl scale –replica = 3 tomcat.yaml
```

kubectl set image − It updates the image of a pod template.

```
$ kubectl set image (-f FILENAME | TYPE NAME)
CONTAINER_NAME_1 = CONTAINER_IMAGE_1 ...
CONTAINER_NAME_N = CONTAINER_IMAGE_N
$ kubectl set image deployment/tomcat busybox = busybox nginx =
nginx:1.9.1
$ kubectl set image deployments, rc tomcat = tomcat6.0 --all
```

kubectl set resources — It is used to set the content of the resource. It updates resource/limits on object with pod template.

```
$ kubectl set resources (-f FILENAME | TYPE NAME) ([--limits = LIMITS
& --
requests = REQUESTS]
$ kubectl set resources deployment tomcat -c = tomcat --
limits = cpu = 200m,memory = 512Mi
```

kubectl top node — It displays CPU/Memory/Storage usage. The top command allows you to see the resource consumption for nodes.

```
$ kubectl top node [node Name]
```

The same command can be used with a pod as well.

CREATING AN APP

In order to create an application for Kubernetes deployment, we need to first create the application on the Docker. This can be done in two ways −

- By downloading
- From Docker file

By Downloading

The existing image can be downloaded from Docker hub and can be stored on the local Docker registry.

In order to do that, run the Docker pull command.

$ docker pull --help

```
Usage: docker pull [OPTIONS] NAME[:TAG|@DIGEST]
Pull an image or a repository from the registry
  -a, --all-tags = false    Download all tagged images in the repository
  --help = false            Print usage
```

Following will be the output of the above code.

```
docker@boot2docker:~$ docker images
REPOSITORY                          TAG        IMAGE ID        CREATED        VIRTUAL SIZE
tacadmins/puppetmaster              latest     0f8b343820fc    5 weeks ago    599.5 MB
<none>                              <none>     daa3212988bf    3 months ago   166.2 MB
busybox                             latest     9967c5ad88de    3 months ago   1.093 MB
ubuntu                              latest     426844ebf7f7    3 months ago   127.1 MB
mattermost/mattermost-preview       latest     2bca39df81ec    4 months ago   453.3 MB
hello-world                         latest     f0cb9bdcaa69    6 months ago   1.848 kB
```

The above screenshot shows a set of images which are stored in our local Docker registry.

If we want to build a container from the image which consists of an application to test, we can do it using the Docker run command.

```
$ docker run −i −t unbunt /bin/bash
```

From Docker File

In order to create an application from the Docker file, we need to first create a Docker file.

Following is an example of Jenkins Docker file.

```
FROM ubuntu:14.04
MAINTAINER vipinkumarmishra@virtusapolaris.com
ENV REFRESHED_AT 2017-01-15
RUN apt-get update -qq && apt-get install -qqy curl
RUN curl https://get.docker.io/gpg | apt-key add -
RUN echo deb http://get.docker.io/ubuntu docker main > /etc/apt/↵
sources.list.d/docker.list
RUN apt-get update -qq && apt-get install -qqy iptables ca-↵
certificates lxc openjdk-6-jdk git-core lxc-docker
ENV JENKINS_HOME /opt/jenkins/data
ENV JENKINS_MIRROR http://mirrors.jenkins-ci.org
RUN mkdir -p $JENKINS_HOME/plugins
RUN curl -sf -o /opt/jenkins/jenkins.war -L $JENKINS_MIRROR/war-↵
stable/latest/jenkins.war
RUN for plugin in chucknorris greenballs scm-api git-client git ↵
ws-cleanup ;\
do curl -sf -o $JENKINS_HOME/plugins/${plugin}.hpi \
-L $JENKINS_MIRROR/plugins/${plugin}/latest/${plugin}.hpi ↵
; done
ADD ./dockerjenkins.sh /usr/local/bin/dockerjenkins.sh
RUN chmod +x /usr/local/bin/dockerjenkins.sh
VOLUME /var/lib/docker
EXPOSE 8080
ENTRYPOINT [ "/usr/local/bin/dockerjenkins.sh" ]
```

Once the above file is created, save it with the name of Dockerfile and cd to the file path. Then, run the following command.

```
docker@boot2docker:~$ docker build --help

Usage: docker build [OPTIONS] PATH | URL | -

Build a new image from the source code at PATH

  -c, --cpu-shares=0       CPU shares (relative weight)
  --cgroup-parent=         Optional parent cgroup for the container
  --cpu-period=0           Limit the CPU CFS (Completely Fair Scheduler) period
  --cpu-quota=0            Limit the CPU CFS (Completely Fair Scheduler) quota
  --cpuset-cpus=           CPUs in which to allow execution (0-3, 0,1)
  --cpuset-mems=           MEMs in which to allow execution (0-3, 0,1)
  -f, --file=              Name of the Dockerfile (Default is 'PATH/Dockerfile')
  --force-rm=false         Always remove intermediate containers
  --help=false             Print usage
  -m, --memory=            Memory limit
  --memory-swap=           Total memory (memory + swap), '-1' to disable swap
  --no-cache=false         Do not use cache when building the image
  --pull=false             Always attempt to pull a newer version of the image
  -q, --quiet=false        Suppress the verbose output generated by the containers
  --rm=true                Remove intermediate containers after a successful build
  -t, --tag=               Repository name (and optionally a tag) for the image
```

```
$ sudo docker build -t jamtur01/Jenkins .
```

Once the image is built, we can test if the image is working fine and can be converted to a container.

```
$ docker run -i -t jamtur01/Jenkins /bin/bash
```

64

APP DEPLOYMENT

Deployment is a method of converting images to containers and then allocating those images to pods in the Kubernetes cluster. This also helps in setting up the application cluster which includes deployment of service, pod, replication controller and replica set. The cluster can be set up in such a way that the applications deployed on the pod can communicate with each other.

In this setup, we can have a load balancer setting on top of one application diverting traffic to a set of pods and later they communicate to backend pods. The communication between pods happen via the service object built in Kubernetes.

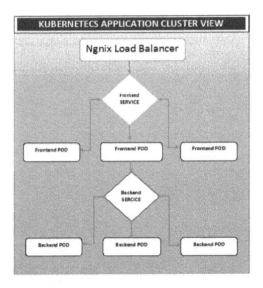

Ngnix Load Balancer Yaml File

```
apiVersion: v1
kind: Service
metadata:
  name: oppv-dev-nginx
  labels:
```

```
      k8s-app: omni-ppv-api
spec:
  type: NodePort
  ports:
  - port: 8080
    nodePort: 31999
    name: omninginx
  selector:
    k8s-app: appname
    component: nginx
    env: dev
```

Nginx Replication Controller Yaml

```
apiVersion: v1
kind: ReplicationController
metadata:
  name: appname
spec:
  replicas: replica_count
  template:
    metadata:
      name: appname
      labels:
        k8s-app: appname
        component: nginx
        env: env_name
spec:
  nodeSelector:
    resource-group: oppv
  containers:
    - name: appname
    image: IMAGE_TEMPLATE
    imagePullPolicy: Always
    ports:
      - containerPort: 8080
      resources:
        requests:
          memory: "request_mem"
          cpu: "request_cpu"
        limits:
          memory: "limit_mem"
          cpu: "limit_cpu"
        env:
        - name: BACKEND_HOST
          value: oppv-env_name-node:3000
```

Frontend Service Yaml File

```yaml
apiVersion: v1
kind: Service
metadata:
  name: appname
  labels:
    k8s-app: appname
spec:
  type: NodePort
  ports:
  - name: http
    port: 3000
    protocol: TCP
    targetPort: 3000
  selector:
    k8s-app: appname
    component: nodejs
    env: dev
```

Frontend Replication Controller Yaml File

```yaml
apiVersion: v1
kind: ReplicationController
metadata:
  name: Frontend
spec:
  replicas: 3
  template:
    metadata:
      name: frontend
      labels:
        k8s-app: Frontend
        component: nodejs
        env: Dev
spec:
  nodeSelector:
    resource-group: oppv
  containers:
    - name: appname
      image: IMAGE_TEMPLATE
      imagePullPolicy: Always
      ports:
        - containerPort: 3000
        resources:
          requests:
            memory: "request_mem"
            cpu: "limit_cpu"
```

67

```
        limits:
          memory: "limit_mem"
          cpu: "limit_cpu"
      env:
        - name: ENV
        valueFrom:
        configMapKeyRef:
        name: appname
        key: config-env
```

Backend Service Yaml File

```
apiVersion: v1
kind: Service
metadata:
  name: backend
  labels:
    k8s-app: backend
spec:
  type: NodePort
  ports:
  - name: http
    port: 9010
    protocol: TCP
    targetPort: 9000
  selector:
    k8s-app: appname
    component: play
    env: dev
```

Backed Replication Controller Yaml File

```
apiVersion: v1
kind: ReplicationController
metadata:
  name: backend
spec:
  replicas: 3
  template:
    metadata:
      name: backend
    labels:
      k8s-app: beckend
      component: play
      env: dev
  spec:
```

```yaml
nodeSelector:
  resource-group: oppv
containers:
  - name: appname
    image: IMAGE_TEMPLATE
    imagePullPolicy: Always
    ports:
    - containerPort: 9000
    command: [ "./docker-entrypoint.sh" ]
    resources:
      requests:
        memory: "request_mem"
        cpu: "request_cpu"
      limits:
        memory: "limit_mem"
        cpu: "limit_cpu"
    volumeMounts:
      - name: config-volume
      mountPath: /app/vipin/play/conf
volumes:
  - name: config-volume
  configMap:
    name: appname
```

AUTOSCALING

Autoscaling is one of the key features in Kubernetes cluster. It is a feature in which the cluster is capable of increasing the number of nodes as the demand for service response increases and decrease the number of nodes as the requirement decreases. This feature of auto scaling is currently supported in Google Cloud Engine (GCE) and Google Container Engine (GKE) and will start with AWS pretty soon.

In order to set up scalable infrastructure in GCE, we need to first have an active GCE project with features of Google cloud monitoring, google cloud logging, and stackdriver enabled.

First, we will set up the cluster with few nodes running in it. Once done, we need to set up the following environment variable.

Environment Variable

```
export NUM_NODES = 2
export KUBE_AUTOSCALER_MIN_NODES = 2
export KUBE_AUTOSCALER_MAX_NODES = 5
export KUBE_ENABLE_CLUSTER_AUTOSCALER = true
```

Once done, we will start the cluster by running kube-up.sh. This will create a cluster together with cluster auto-scalar add on.

```
./cluster/kube-up.sh
```

On creation of the cluster, we can check our cluster using the following kubectl command.

```
$ kubectl get nodes
NAME                          STATUS                    AGE
kubernetes-master             Ready,SchedulingDisabled  10m
kubernetes-minion-group-de5q  Ready                     10m
kubernetes-minion-group-yhdx  Ready                     8m
```

Now, we can deploy an application on the cluster and then enable the horizontal pod autoscaler. This can be done using the following command.

```
$ kubectl autoscale deployment <Application Name> --cpu-percent = 50 --
min = 1 --
max = 10
```

The above command shows that we will maintain at least one and maximum 10 replica of the POD as the load on the application increases.

We can check the status of autoscaler by running the $kubclt get hpa command. We will increase the load on the pods using the following command.

```
$ kubectl run -i --tty load-generator --image = busybox /bin/sh
$ while true; do wget -q -O- http://php-apache.default.svc.cluster.local; done
```

We can check the hpa by running $ kubectl get hpa command.

```
$ kubectl get hpa
NAME       REFERENCE                  TARGET CURRENT
php-apache  Deployment/php-apache/scale   50%    310%

MINPODS MAXPODS  AGE
  1       20     2m

$ kubectl get deployment php-apache
NAME       DESIRED   CURRENT   UP-TO-DATE   AVAILABLE
AGE
php-apache   7         7         7            3        4m
```

We can check the number of pods running using the following command.

```
jsz@jsz-desk2:~/k8s-src$ kubectl get pods
php-apache-2046965998-3ewo6 0/1     Pending 0       1m
php-apache-2046965998-8m03k 1/1     Running 0       1m
php-apache-2046965998-ddpgp 1/1     Running 0       5m
php-apache-2046965998-lnk6 1/1      Running 0       1m
php-apache-2046965998-nj465 0/1     Pending 0       1m
php-apache-2046965998-tmwg1 1/1     Running 0       1m
```

```
php-apache-2046965998-xkbw1 0/1     Pending 0       1m
```

And finally, we can get the node status.

```
$ kubectl get nodes
NAME                          STATUS                  AGE
kubernetes-master             Ready,SchedulingDisabled   9m
kubernetes-minion-group-6z51  Ready                      43s
kubernetes-minion-group-de5q  Ready                      9m
kubernetes-minion-group-yhdx  Ready                      9m
```

DASHBOARD SETUP

Setting up Kubernetes dashboard involves several steps with a set of tools required as the prerequisites to set it up.

- Docker (1.3+)
- go (1.5+)
- nodejs (4.2.2+)
- npm (1.3+)
- java (7+)
- gulp (3.9+)
- Kubernetes (1.1.2+)

Setting Up the Dashboard

```
$ sudo apt-get update && sudo apt-get upgrade
```

Installing Python

```
$ sudo apt-get install python
$ sudo apt-get install python3
```

Installing GCC

```
$ sudo apt-get install gcc-4.8 g++-4.8
```

Installing make

```
$ sudo apt-get install make
```

Installing Java

```
$ sudo apt-get install openjdk-7-jdk
```

nstalling Node.js

```
$ wget https://nodejs.org/dist/v4.2.2/node-v4.2.2.tar.gz
$ tar -xzf node-v4.2.2.tar.gz
$ cd node-v4.2.2
$ ./configure
$ make
$ sudo make install
```

Installing gulp

```
$ npm install -g gulp
$ npm install gulp
```

Verifying Versions

```
Java Version
$ java --version
java version "1.7.0_91"
OpenJDK Runtime Environment (IcedTea 2.6.3) (7u91-2.6.3-
1~deb8u1+rpi1)
OpenJDK Zero VM (build 24.91-b01, mixed mode)

$ node -v
V4.2.2

$ npn -v
2.14.7

$ gulp -v
[09:51:28] CLI version 3.9.0

$ sudo gcc --version
gcc (Raspbian 4.8.4-1) 4.8.4
Copyright (C) 2013 Free Software Foundation, Inc. This is free software;
see the source for copying conditions. There is NO warranty; not even for
MERCHANTABILITY or FITNESS FOR A PARTICULAR PURPOSE.
```

Installing GO

```
$ git clone https://go.googlesource.com/go
$ cd go
$ git checkout go1.4.3
```

```
$ cd src

Building GO
$ ./all.bash
$ vi /root/.bashrc
In the .bashrc
    export GOROOT = $HOME/go
    export PATH = $PATH:$GOROOT/bin

$ go version
go version go1.4.3 linux/arm
```

Installing Kubernetes Dashboard

```
$ git clone https://github.com/kubernetes/dashboard.git
$ cd dashboard
$ npm install -g bower
```

Running the Dashboard

```
$ git clone https://github.com/kubernetes/dashboard.git
$ cd dashboard
$ npm install -g bower
$ gulp serve
[11:19:12] Requiring external module babel-core/register
[11:20:50] Using gulpfile ~/dashboard/gulpfile.babel.js
[11:20:50] Starting 'package-backend-source'...
[11:20:50] Starting 'kill-backend'...
[11:20:50] Finished 'kill-backend' after 1.39 ms
[11:20:50] Starting 'scripts'...
[11:20:53] Starting 'styles'...
[11:21:41] Finished 'scripts' after 50 s
[11:21:42] Finished 'package-backend-source' after 52 s
[11:21:42] Starting 'backend'...
[11:21:43] Finished 'styles' after 49 s
[11:21:43] Starting 'index'...
[11:21:44] Finished 'index' after 1.43 s
[11:21:44] Starting 'watch'...
[11:21:45] Finished 'watch' after 1.41 s
[11:23:27] Finished 'backend' after 1.73 min
[11:23:27] Starting 'spawn-backend'...
[11:23:27] Finished 'spawn-backend' after 88 ms
[11:23:27] Starting 'serve'...
2016/02/01 11:23:27 Starting HTTP server on port 9091
2016/02/01 11:23:27 Creating API client for
2016/02/01 11:23:27 Creating Heapster REST client for
http://localhost:8082
```

```
[11:23:27] Finished 'serve' after 312 ms
[BS] [BrowserSync SPA] Running...
[BS] Access URLs:
 --------------------------------------
 Local: http://localhost:9090/
 External: http://192.168.1.21:9090/
 --------------------------------------
 UI: http://localhost:3001
 UI External: http://192.168.1.21:3001
 --------------------------------------
[BS] Serving files from: /root/dashboard/.tmp/serve
[BS] Serving files from: /root/dashboard/src/app/frontend
[BS] Serving files from: /root/dashboard/src/app
```

MONITORING

Monitoring is one of the key component for managing large clusters. For this, we have a number of tools.

Monitoring with Prometheus

It is a monitoring and alerting system. It was built at SoundCloud and was open sourced in 2012. It handles the multi-dimensional data very well.

Prometheus has multiple components to participate in monitoring −

- Prometheus − It is the core component that scraps and stores data.

- Prometheus node explore − Gets the host level matrices and exposes them to Prometheus.

- Ranch-eye − is an haproxy and exposes cAdvisor stats to Prometheus.

- Grafana − Visualization of data.

- InfuxDB − Time series database specifically used to store data from rancher.

- Prom-ranch-exporter − It is a simple node.js application, which helps in querying Rancher server for the status of stack of service.

Sematext Docker Agent

It is a modern Docker-aware metrics, events, and log collection agent. It runs as a tiny container on every Docker host and collects logs, metrics, and events for all cluster node and containers. It discovers all containers (one pod might contain multiple containers) including containers for Kubernetes core services, if the core services are deployed in Docker containers. After its deployment, all logs and metrics are immediately available out of the box.

Deploying Agents to Nodes

Kubernetes provides DeamonSets which ensures pods are added to the cluster.

Configuring SemaText Docker Agent

It is configured via environment variables.

- Get a free account at apps.sematext.com, if you don't have one already.

- Create an SPM App of type "Docker" to obtain the SPM App Token. SPM App will hold your Kubernetes performance metrics and event.

- Create a Logsene App to obtain the Logsene App Token. Logsene App will hold your Kubernetes logs.

- Edit values of LOGSENE_TOKEN and SPM_TOKEN in the DaemonSet definition as shown below.

  - Grab the latest sematext-agent-daemonset.yml (raw plain-text) template (also shown below).

  - Store it somewhere on the disk.

  - Replace the SPM_TOKEN and LOGSENE_TOKEN placeholders with your SPM and Logsene App tokens.

Create DaemonSet Object

```
apiVersion: extensions/v1beta1
kind: DaemonSet
metadata:
  name: sematext-agent
spec:
  template:
    metadata:
      labels:
        app: sematext-agent
    spec:
      selector: {}
      dnsPolicy: "ClusterFirst"
      restartPolicy: "Always"
      containers:
      - name: sematext-agent
        image: sematext/sematext-agent-docker:latest
        imagePullPolicy: "Always"
        env:
        - name: SPM_TOKEN
          value: "REPLACE THIS WITH YOUR SPM TOKEN"
        - name: LOGSENE_TOKEN
          value: "REPLACE THIS WITH YOUR LOGSENE TOKEN"
        - name: KUBERNETES
          value: "1"
        volumeMounts:
          - mountPath: /var/run/docker.sock
            name: docker-sock
          - mountPath: /etc/localtime
            name: localtime
        volumes:
          - name: docker-sock
            hostPath:
              path: /var/run/docker.sock
          - name: localtime
            hostPath:
              path: /etc/localtime
```

Running the Sematext Agent Docker with kubectl

```
$ kubectl create -f sematext-agent-daemonset.yml
daemonset "sematext-agent-daemonset" created
```

Kubernetes Log

Kubernetes containers' logs are not much different from Docker container logs. However, Kubernetes users need to view logs for the deployed pods. Hence, it is very useful to have Kubernetes-specific information available for log search, such as —

- Kubernetes namespace
- Kubernetes pod name
- Kubernetes container name
- Docker image name
- Kubernetes UID

Using ELK Stack and LogSpout

ELK stack includes Elasticsearch, Logstash, and Kibana. To collect and forward the logs to the logging platform, we will use LogSpout (though there are other options such as FluentD).

The following code shows how to set up ELK cluster on Kubernetes and create service for ElasticSearch —

```
apiVersion: v1
kind: Service
metadata:
  name: elasticsearch
  namespace: elk
  labels:
    component: elasticsearch
spec:
  type: LoadBalancer
  selector:
    component: elasticsearch
  ports:
  - name: http
    port: 9200
    protocol: TCP
  - name: transport
    port: 9300
    protocol: TCP
```

Creating Replication Controller

```
apiVersion: v1
kind: ReplicationController
metadata:
  name: es
  namespace: elk
```

```yaml
  labels:
    component: elasticsearch
spec:
  replicas: 1
  template:
    metadata:
      labels:
        component: elasticsearch
spec:
serviceAccount: elasticsearch
containers:
  - name: es
    securityContext:
    capabilities:
    add:
    - IPC_LOCK
  image: quay.io/pires/docker-elasticsearch-kubernetes:1.7.1-4
  env:
  - name: KUBERNETES_CA_CERTIFICATE_FILE
  value: /var/run/secrets/kubernetes.io/serviceaccount/ca.crt
  - name: NAMESPACE
  valueFrom:
    fieldRef:
      fieldPath: metadata.namespace
  - name: "CLUSTER_NAME"
    value: "myesdb"
  - name: "DISCOVERY_SERVICE"
    value: "elasticsearch"
  - name: NODE_MASTER
    value: "true"
  - name: NODE_DATA
    value: "true"
  - name: HTTP_ENABLE
    value: "true"
ports:
- containerPort: 9200
  name: http
  protocol: TCP
- containerPort: 9300
volumeMounts:
- mountPath: /data
  name: storage
volumes:
  - name: storage
    emptyDir: {}
```

Kibana URL

For Kibana, we provide the Elasticsearch URL as an environment variable.

```
- name: KIBANA_ES_URL
value: "http://elasticsearch.elk.svc.cluster.local:9200"
- name: KUBERNETES_TRUST_CERT
value: "true"
```

Kibana UI will be reachable at container port 5601 and corresponding host/Node Port combination. When you begin, there won't be any data in Kibana (which is expected as you have not pushed any data).